Bossy the Bunny
At School

Pamela Griffiths

First Published 2018as

Book 3

Bossy the Bunny

At School

ISBN-10: 1717078222
ISBN-13: 978-1717078223

Classification: Children's Rhyming Story

Website pamelagriffiths.com
Twitter @pamg50
Facebook Author Pamela Griffiths page

Bossy the bunny
At Easter

Book 1 in the Bossy the Bunny series

Five star review on amazon.co.uk

Bossy the Bunny
The Birthday

Book 2 in the Bossy the Bunny series

Bossy The Bunny
At School

Bossy the bunny is clever

He attends the rabbit school

He has learned how to do things

Because he is nobody's fool

Bossy goes to school each day

Along with all the others

He listens to the teacher

There is so much to discover

Bossy likes his teacher

She is very smart

She knows just about everything

She teaches it from the heart

She teaches bunnies how to survive

And teaches them how to play

She shows them how to spot danger

And when they should hop away

Their teacher is called Miss Hopper

She passes on all her skills

Miss Hopper has a classroom

In a clearing in the hills

The bunnies come from all around

To attend the school each day

When the bell rings at the end

They leave and hop away

Miss Hopper has a few helpers

To help her in the classroom

There are so many bunnies

She may need more helpers soon

When the sun is rising

The school always rings a bell

This is to let the bunnies know

'It's school time' they all yell

The lessons are all exciting

Miss Hopper makes sure they are

Nature is a wonderful thing

'If you're good you will get a gold star'

There is so much to teach them

The bunnies are still very young

Miss Hopper warns them of the wasps

She doesn't want them to get stung

'What does two and two make?' Miss Hopper
asks

'Four' The bunnies shout out loud

'Well done' Miss Hopper says

'You have made me very proud'

The bell rings now its playtime

In the fields they jump

They are very happy

As they jump and land with a thump

Back in the classroom it's story time

Miss Hopper tells them a tale

About a rabbit that ran away

And was swallowed by a big whale

She told them that the rabbit

Was saved and free from harm

Whale coughed and the rabbit popped out

He escaped as the sea was calm

The bunnies liked the stories

They were always so much fun

Bossy liked the stories too

Remembered them when they had done

The bunnies acted out the stories

It was always good to pretend

They didn't want the stories

To ever come to the end

'Tomorrow we will sing'

Miss Hopper told the class

'We can make some instruments'

'We can sing and dance in the grass'

Bossy liked the music

He loved to dance around

When the sun was shining brightly

Birds added their own special sound

Soon it would be home time

The bunnies would go home

Bossy loved his bunny friends

He would never be alone

Miss Hopper gave them home work

They had to learn a rhyme

At school the next day

They had memorised each line

The school bell rang

It was time for them to go

They were taught so much today

But there is still much more to know

Bossy played with the others

They all had lots of fun

Lots of things for them to do

Before the setting of the sun

Today had been a good day

Now it's time to go to sleep

Bossy was given a lovely gold star

It was his award to keep

The sun was rising in the sky

The school bell rang again

It was time to go to school

Today In the pouring rain

Miss Hopper told the class

'We will stay inside today'

'I will tell you all a story'

'Until the rain has gone away'

Soon the sun came out again

The rain had now stopped falling

The school bell rang for play time

'It's playtime' Bossy was calling'

Bossy and his friends were lucky

They had a school to attend

A place where they were taught

Until school days come to an end

The bunnies would always remember

What was taught to them in the schools

Soon they would all become adults

Remembering Miss Hoppers rules

Happy schooldays

The End

Dedication

For my partner Sandy Hoffman
And my family and friends

For the children who have enjoyed this
story and the adults who have enjoyed reading
this book to them.

Thank you

Pamela Griffiths

For more information about Sheffield author
Pamela Griffiths
(National Award winning poet and author)

Please check out these sites.

Website www.pamelagriffiths.com

Twitter (@pamg56) https://twitter.com/Pamg56

Facebook Author page
https://m.facebook.com/Author-Pamela-Griffiths-
167707173288865/

Amazon.co.uk
https://www.amazon.co.uk/Pamela-
Griffiths/e/B0034ODJVQ/ref=ntt_dp_epwbk_0